BE MORE OLIVIA

CONTENTS

LIVE CREATIVELY..4
Olivia's creativity has earned her two smash-hit albums and millions of fans. Learn to embrace your originality and talent, whatever it may be, the Rodrigo way.

OWN YOUR VULNERABILITY 16
When it's feeling especially brutal in the world, it's easy to withdraw from your loved ones out of fear—but it's Olivia's raw vulnerability that draws fans in and makes them feel seen.

BE GUTSY..28
It's taken bravery for Olivia to put herself out there from such a young age and have the strength to speak up about what she believes in—learn to be as gutsy as her, even when it's scary.

SURROUND YOURSELF WITH LOVE 40
Olivia understands that whether it's going through heartbreak or navigating life's inevitable changes, it's always easier with your besties by your side.

JUST BE YOU!... 52
Olivia can be consumed by 'jealousy, jealousy' and writes about not feeling perfect enough. But it's her unique persona that we love! Embrace who you really are, and you'll find your people.

INTRODUCTION

From the moment 17-year-old Olivia Rodrigo burst onto the pop scene with her razor-sharp debut single, 'driver's license', we knew that this was a generation-defining superstar making her mark.

Today, Olivia has truly earned her place at the top of the pop-girl hall of fame—and not just because she possesses a unique talent to smash both a moving piano ballad and a punky girl-rock anthem.

We love her because she's brutally honest, emotionally intelligent, effortlessly witty, and wise beyond her years.

As she progressed from Disney child-star to Grammy-winning darling and Glastonbury headliner, Olivia has honed her craft, and maintained her sense of self, while keeping her chunky boots rooted firmly on planet Earth.

There's so much we can learn from Olivia—from how she finds creative inspiration, to what motivates her to do good in the world, to what she prioritizes for a happy, fulfilling life. Read on for 25 ways to be more Olivia.

DISCLAIMER
This book has not been written or endorsed by Olivia Rodrigo. It was created for Livies, by Livies. It is a love letter to Olivia and all those who feel a connection to her.

CHAPTER 1

LIVE

CREATIVELY

Whether you choose drawing or dancing, writing or music, you'll know that making art is a magical feeling—even if it never sees the light of day. It helps us enter a "flow" state where nothing and nobody else matters. Many of us tell ourselves that we're not creative, but creativity lives in all of us. As Olivia demonstrates, all we have to do is stay open, lean in, and trust the process.

"I was always singing. I was always super motivated to do things."

Live Creatively

FOLLOW YOUR CURIOSITY

Few people know exactly what their future will look like when they're only six years old. As kids, we dream up implausible and fantastical futures for ourselves—and a little Olivia Rodrigo, born in Temecula, California, was no different. Initially, she dreamed of becoming an Olympic gymnast, but when she started acting and piano lessons, it became clear that her parents had a tiny star on their hands. It was Olivia who insisted they drive her to auditions in LA, somehow understanding that she was destined for bright lights. "I have no idea why I was like 'this is what I want to do'", she said—but she was right to pursue it, because she eventually secured a starring role on the Disney show, *Bizaardvark*. If a 12-year-old Olivia could trust her intuition and follow her passions, then we can all strive to do the same.

"I'm really inspired by vintage things and I'm obsessed with the nineties."

Live Creatively

INSPIRATION IS EVERYWHERE

Olivia lives by a "bible" that goes by the name of *Big Magic* by Elizabeth Gilbert. Gilbert describes ideas as independent entities, which seek out the people who are most open to them. She says that inspiration isn't something you can control or force; rather, you have to welcome it and follow it wherever it goes. It's clear that Olivia has taken this wisdom to heart, inviting ideas and welcoming inspiration into her life with open arms. A diary entry about driving around crying led to her first hit, 'driver's license'. Watching classic noughties movies like *Jennifer's Body* and *The Princess Diaries* led to the revenge-plot music video for 'good 4 u'. A joke with a friend led to her tongue-in-cheek single, 'bad idea, right?'. Remember: the most creative ideas can strike at any time and from anywhere. You just have to be willing to reach out and grab them.

"Sometimes good songs come from discipline and the craft of songwriting."

Live Creatively

WORK HARD

Yes, ideas can strike when you least expect them. But that's not where the story ends. You need the work ethic, perseverance, and patience to take that idea and transform it into something special. You can also make inspiration for yourself by simply sitting down and getting started. Olivia teaches us that creativity isn't solely something you possess, it's also something you *do*. It's an action. It's a verb. During the Covid-19 lockdowns, she committed to sitting down at her piano every day to write songs—a discipline that honed her craft and resulted in her Grammy-winning debut album, *Sour*. It's an important reminder that success doesn't come from talent and luck alone, but from showing up and making it happen.

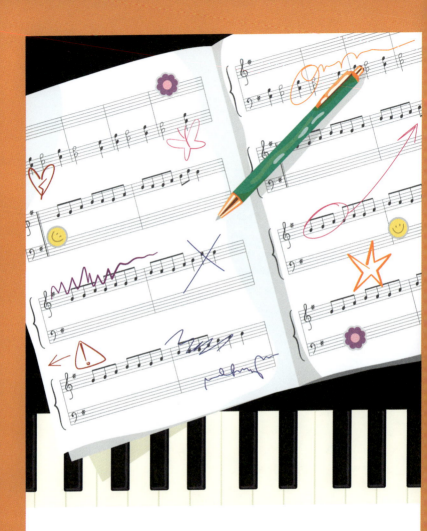

"You're never gonna learn from something if you throw it away the second you think it's not good."

Live Creatively

FINISHED IS BETTER THAN PERFECT

In creative pursuits (and in life), you sometimes have to take three steps backwards in order to take one step forwards. When making each of her albums, Olivia wrote plenty of songs that were left on the cutting room floor and will likely never see the light of day. But it's okay to make something imperfect (and maybe even bad), because at least you've still produced something—and you'll take valuable lessons from everything you create. In the same way, you might think something isn't working, but then you can seek input from your closest artistic collaborator (for example, the producer Dan Nigro, Olivia's main collaborator on both *Sour* and *Guts*), and you can push through the discomfort and insecurity of getting something "wrong", until eventually you get it right. The magic of creativity lies in embracing imperfection—and trying, and trying again.

> **Make art with absolutely no intention of it ever being consumed... do it for the love of it.**

Live Creatively

DO IT FOR YOU

Olivia might release smash-hit singles and multi-award-winning albums, and she might perform in front of thousands of fans at her electrifying concerts. But none of that would be possible without the teenage girl who sat in her room writing music about her feelings, simply because she loved it. When writing her sophomore album, she admits she felt pressure to make something as groundbreaking and well-loved as her debut. "I really had to block out the noise, and focus on the craft of songwriting," she said. Nothing stifles originality quite like worrying what other people will think. So, create for the sake of it. Do it for yourself. Think about what you'd like to listen to, or look at, or watch, or wear—and work from there, because that is art in the freest, most authentic sense. And if the outcome is a banger that thousands of people will scream from the top of their lungs in an arena—well, consider that a happy bonus.

CHAPTER 2
OWN YOUR VULNERABILITY

Being human means being messy (yes, even global pop superstars). It means we all feel insecure, angry, resentful, jealous, and heartbroken sometimes. It truly is brutal living in this world. But as uncomfortable as it might be, your vulnerability is your superpower. When you wear your heart on your sleeve, you connect to others in beautiful ways.

"I needed to write those songs to process those emotions."

Own Your Vulnerability

GET TO KNOW YOURSELF

It's totally normal to feel all the feelings—especially when you're a teenager who has just watched her ex-boyfriend move on with "that blonde girl". The best way to process those big scary emotions? Let. Them. Out. Maybe that's speaking to your best friend. Maybe that's seeing a therapist. Maybe that's writing a heart-wrenching ballad. Or maybe it's scribbling everything into the pages of a journal. Alongside writing songs to dissect and process her emotions, Olivia is a big fan of spilling her guts onto the page in a stream of consciousness. "It's nice to look back at issues I thought were gonna be world-ending and be like, 'ah, that worked out totally fine. It made me who I am,'" she said. "It just kind of puts things into perspective." So take a leaf out of Olivia's book. Work through your emotions in order to understand yourself better and learn important lessons for the future.

"If you speak honestly about
any experience, then someone
is going to find truth in it."

Own Your Vulnerability

BE BRUTALLY HONEST

You know that feeling when you've overshared a bit too much and then the next day you're filled with regret? Yep, we've all been there. Vulnerability can make us feel uncomfortable and awkward. We feel shame and worry about being judged. But the best relationships you have are the ones where you can be honest and open about your darkest secrets and deepest fears. Honesty is a shortcut to connection. Olivia is relentlessly truthful in her music, whether that's describing an obsession with her boyfriend's ex, or holding a grudge against someone who wronged her. And that's exactly why we love her, because we've all been there too—she verbalizes what many of us feel too scared to say. When we're honest about how we really feel, other people breathe a sigh of relief. As Olivia says: "Honesty is always relatable. Humans are so much more alike than we are different."

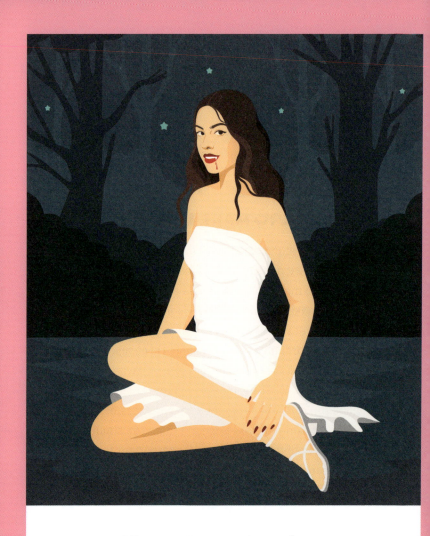

"How am I ever going to learn if I can't make a mistake in the privacy of my own life?"

Own Your Vulnerability

IT'S OK TO MAKE MISTAKES

When you're young, and you're navigating grown-up relationships, friendships, and careers for the first time, you're bound to make some mistakes along the way. In fact, you'll probably make mistakes at every point in your life (sorry!). But that's fine—because if we never make mistakes, we'll never learn anything. Through her songwriting, Olivia acknowledges her missteps, and she grows from them. In 'favorite crime', she recognizes her own role in an unhealthy, toxic relationship. In 'making the bed', she faces the consequences of her own actions. But making mistakes doesn't mean we should beat ourselves up until the end of time. It's important to forgive ourselves too. Speak to yourself in the same way you'd speak to a friend: "Sure, you messed up. But I still love you regardless."

"You can't make art and have a good career if you're not there."

Own Your Vulnerability

PRIORITIZE YOUR MENTAL HEALTH

Being a global sensation is hard work. One minute you're in the recording studio, the next you're on a tour bus, on stage, in an interview, at an awards ceremony… it really never stops, and it can be hard to take time for yourself. Of course, most of us will never live such a glamorous, high-octane lifestyle. But still, we all have tons of commitments and responsibilities, and we can easily send ourselves into a downward mental spiral if we're not careful. Yes, we all want to do the best we possibly can in all aspects of our lives—but, as Olivia says: "An empty pitcher can't pour." You can't achieve your wildest dreams (and have the time of your life) if you're not also resting and taking care of yourself. The trick is to find your own happy place. Olivia finds peace by knitting, baking, and spending as much time as possible in the water (like a typical Pisces). We all need to create space to remove the pressure and just *be*.

"If I never endured any heartbreak in my life, I wouldn't be half the person I am today and I wouldn't know myself nearly as well."

Own Your Vulnerability

EVERY HEARTBREAK MAKES YOU STRONGER

Few things hurt more than a broken heart. But when you have to pick up all the tiny pieces of your heart that are scattered across the floor, you confront who you really are and what you're truly made of. Olivia's first breakup left her questioning why she wasn't enough for that person, and it left her self-esteem in tatters. But from her darkest low, she built something incredible: an award-winning album, and a fanbase that relates to every word she sings. She made songs that will outlast the pain that relationship left her with—and now those songs belong to all of us, too. With each heartbreak, we learn so much. We learn the warning signs we might have overlooked. We learn that we still have value and worth, and someday we will be more than enough for a romantic partner. When you finally fix your broken heart, you might just discover that it's bigger and fuller of love than ever before.

CHAPTER 3

BE

GUTSY

Living like Olivia Rodrigo takes bravery and courage. It takes guts. And that's not only because she overcomes stage fright to perform in front of gigantic crowds—although, that's extremely impressive. It's because she says what needs to be said, and she fights for what's right. Being bold is scary—but it's the only way to change the world for the better.

"I think you need a little delusion to get by. It's just hope, you know."

Be Gutsy

NEVER GIVE UP ON YOUR DREAMS

In some ways, Olivia Rodrigo became an adult before her time. Working as an actor on *Bizaardvark* and then *High School Musical: The Musical: The Series*, she learned how to hold her own in rooms full of suits from the tender age of 12. So when it came to making music for the first time, she knew what she wanted and she knew how to ask for it. Instead of signing to Disney's in-house label like many of her predecessors, she chose to sign with Interscope/Geffen because they respected her songwriting skills. And although the original plan was to release an EP (Extended Play), Olivia convinced her record label that she was ready to make her debut album, *Sour*—and she was absolutely right. Only you will truly know what your dreams are, and what it will take to turn them into reality. You just need the guts to go out there and do it. So, what are you waiting for?

"I would love, if I was a little girl,
to see someone stand up for future-me
like [I did at Glastonbury]."

Be Gutsy

RAISE YOUR VOICE

It's June 24th 2022, and the news has just broken that Roe v Wade—the ruling that had established abortion as a federal right in the USA—has been overturned. A 19-year-old Olivia is devastated by the rollback of women's reproductive rights, but she's due to perform at Glastonbury festival (the UK's biggest and most iconic music festival) the next day, and bring out British pop icon Lily Allen on stage to duet her classic hit, 'F*** You'. So what does heartbroken Liv do? She decides to get loud. "I'm devastated and terrified, and so many women and girls are going to die because of this," she shouts to the electric Glasto crowd, before dedicating Lily's scathing song to each member of the Supreme Court who voted to overturn the ruling. The roaring crowd sings along, with middle fingers flipped, in an act of sour rebellion. Since then, Olivia has consistently spoken up about women's reproductive rights. In doing so, she reminds other women that they matter. Their bodies belong to them. They aren't alone.

> **I always try to do the right thing, even if it's the hard thing.**

Be Gutsy

DO GOOD

Sharing your talents with other people is an act of generosity in itself. Making art that people will resonate with and creating a space for people to have fun and let loose, is one incredible way of being the good you want to see in the world. But Olivia takes it a step further than that. On her Guts Tour, she donated a portion of the proceeds from ticket sales to her Fund 4 Good, a global initiative to support community-based non-profits that champion women's education, support reproductive rights, and fight against gender-based violence. But philanthropy doesn't need to happen on such a large scale. You can do your bit by buying food for someone in need, setting yourself a challenge and fundraising for a charity that matters to you, or even just supporting a friend. When you do good 4 others, you do good 4 u.

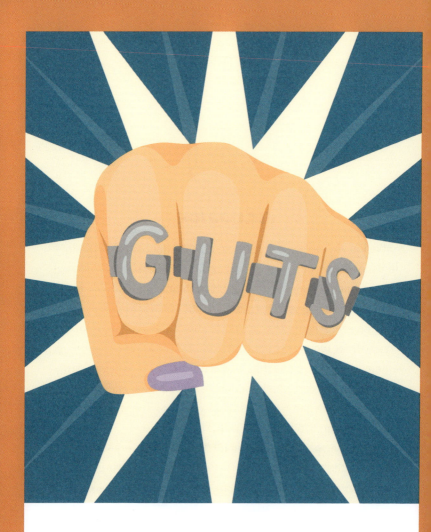

"You can be proud of yourself and also keep working hard at things, and also be humble, and be so grateful, and also be so privileged."

Be Gutsy

FEEL PRIDE

We know that Olivia is just like us. She doubts herself and feels insecure, and sometimes laments how socially awkward and "tragic" she can be (although we highly doubt that's true). But she has also achieved an awful lot in her young life, and she refuses to downplay these incredible achievements. "As women, we feel that if we're like 'I did this amazing thing,' we feel ashamed to say that, or we want to be small constantly," Olivia said. Instead, she believes we can acknowledge multiple truths at the same time: when we succeed at something, we can recognize that luck and privilege played a role, while also congratulating ourselves for all the hard work we put in, and all the amazing steps we took to shape our destinies. If we do that, we show others that they are also worthy of celebration. It's not arrogant, but empowering, to give yourself a pat on the back.

"I'm so proud of my generation and the way that people have come together and not put up with the bulls*** that has been put up with for so many years."

Be Gutsy

BREAK FREE

When the song 'all-american bitch' opens the album *Guts*, you don't know what's coming. In a higher octave, Olivia sings soothingly about being the perfect woman; a ray of sunshine who looks the part, and who happily goes along with what everyone else wants. And then—bam! A crescendo of drums and guitar, and the chorus transforms into a punky, shouty anthem. The contrast throughout the song confronts the expectations that are placed on women, and the rage that can live alongside these pressures. In this way, it acts as a rallying call: to express your anger and dissatisfaction, to break free from the limiting identities that keep us trapped. Olivia reminds us that it's okay to be soft and hard, sweet and dissatisfied, grateful and annoyed. No one else gets to define who you are and what you should be—except for you.

CHAPTER 4

SURROUND YOURSELF

WITH LOVE

We all need people we can go to and ask: "this is a bad idea, right?" And when we go and do the bad idea anyway, they'll message us and say "hope ur ok." The right people—who look out for our best interests and inspire us—can help us to become our best selves.

"I'm a big 'quality over quantity' person when it comes to friends."

Surround Yourself With Love

PRIORITIZE FRIENDSHIP

Sometimes the great love stories of our time become romantic songs, or heart-wrenching breakup ballads. And other times, the most consistent and beautiful love stories don't get the credit they deserve—because they're the ones we share with our friends. Olivia, thankfully, respects the role her closest pals have played in her life, including actress Iris Apatow, fellow popstar Conan Gray, and her co-star from *Bizaardvark*, Madison Hu. "All of my female friendships have been so much more fulfilling than any relationship that I've ever had," she has said. "They're so much more fun and I've learned so much more about myself." Of Madison, Olivia has said "She's literally my soul mate," and clearly the feeling is mutual. "Our friendship has taught me how to approach almost every other relationship in my life," Madison has said. No matter which direction you take in life, your best friends should always be there to ground you, make you laugh, and cheer you on.

"I have a really wonderful support system around me... I don't know what I would do without that."

Surround Yourself With Love

LEAN ON YOUR PEOPLE

As an only child, Olivia is lucky to have an awesome relationship with her parents. "I'm best friends with my parents, and I got so much attention growing up," she has said. But even if you don't have family members to rely on, the beauty of growing up is that you get to choose your family.

Liv now has plenty of people she goes to for advice and support—and sometimes even some tough love. One of those people is her producer and main collaborator, Dan Nigro.

"I love Dan because he is so honest with me," she said. "He cares about me enough to be like, 'you can do better than that.'" When life is as chaotic and overwhelming as it can be, we all need those people who can cut through the BS and see us for who we really are, what we really want, and know best how to support us and push us to do better. Think about who those people are in your life—and hold them close.

"Those who mind don't matter,
and those who matter don't mind."

Surround Yourself With Love

STOP PEOPLE-PLEASING

It's normal to want to be liked, respected, and validated by people. But there are billions of people in the world, and it's simply impossible to be liked, respected, and validated by everyone. This is why trying to please everyone, all of the time, is a losing battle. Like every hard-working empath, Olivia has admitted to having people-pleasing tendencies in the past, but "I'm working on it," she said. Overcoming people-pleasing isn't about ignoring what anyone thinks and just steam-rolling through life. It's about only trying to please the people who you really respect, and who love you, rather than trying to win the favor of those who will never understand. And, even then, you must always keep in mind what you want, and trust that you know what's best for you.

"I think [Chappell Roan] is one of the most singular, inspiring, powerful artists I've ever had the pleasure of meeting."

Surround Yourself With Love

LIFT OTHERS UP

They say that it's lonely at the top—but Olivia has a great solution for that. She loves to champion other artists and pull them up the ladder of pop super-stardom with her. When she covered Noah Kahan's 'Stick Season' in London on BBC Radio 1's Live Lounge, describing him as an "incredible songwriter," he understandably freaked out (his words). She was also one of the first people to shout from the rooftops about a certain pop sensation named Chappell Roan, inviting her to open for the first leg of her Guts Tour, and later bringing her on stage to perform Chappell's hit, 'HOT TO GO!'. With great success comes a great opportunity: you have a platform to promote and spotlight the people you think are amazing. And anyway, when you share the stage and the glory, it's a hell of a lot more fun.

> I'm so happy being alone in my house watching a show or reading a book. That's peak joy.

Surround Yourself With Love

LOVE YOURSELF

It's so important to nurture your relationships with your favorite people—whether that's your romantic partner, your besties, your family, your collaborators, or your fans. But you should never neglect the most important relationship in your life: the one you have with yourself. Despite being on the road and constantly surrounded by people, Olivia makes a very conscious effort to spend time in her own company. In 2023, she set a New Year's resolution to spend more time alone, "and I've definitely done that," she said. Why? Because alone time helps us stay connected to the person we've always been. It offers time to focus on self-care and allows breathing space for those magical ideas to find us. When we reconnect to who we are, we come back to the world even happier than before.

CHAPTER 5

JUST BE

YOU!

There's only one Olivia Rodrigo. As much as we can try to be more Olivia, we can never actually *be* Olivia. It would be a bit weird and worrying if we could! That's no bad thing. We're all completely, utterly, beautifully unique—and it's time we fully embrace that concept. Part of being more Olivia means being more *you*. So just let loose, embrace your imperfections, and never forget how special you are.

"Music is so fun.
It's supposed to be fun."

Just Be You!

HAVE A BALL

It goes without saying: life can be serious. We all have work and responsibilities; we all experience challenges and some degree of suffering. But, generally speaking, life is also deeply unserious if we choose to view it that way. Joy and humor are absolute essentials in Olivia's toolkit, and she goes out of her way to find the silly side. While creating her song 'vampire' with Dan Nigro, she knew she needed to create a "clean version" and replace the phrase "fame f***er" with something more appropriate for kids. And so, she and Dan decided to experiment with a few very unlikely options, including "tree hugger," "whale blubber," and "garlic butter". Of course, none of these phrases would ever make the cut—but who cares if you get side-tracked when you're having a good time? Fill your world with laughter, and life will always be sweeter than it is sour.

Just Be You!

EXIST IN THE REAL WORLD

It's so easy to get sucked into the black hole of social media. Whether that's stalking your ex (we've all been there), or simply scrolling through endless pictures of vacations and cool vintage clothes, the spiral can feel addictive. But Olivia knows that obsessing over other people's lives on social media is a one-way ticket to dissatisfaction. It tricks us into thinking other people's lives are better than ours, when we're only really seeing half the story. Olivia put it best when she said: "Social media is fake, and nobody is as perfect as they seem online." It helps to remember this when you're scrolling through those tiny, curated squares—comparing someone's outsides with your insides isn't a fair fight.

Also, take Liv's lead and stay off social media as much as possible. See your friends IRL. Head out for a walk in nature. Get lost in a great book. Whatever you do, remember that life is for living, not simply watching through a screen.

"If one person is successful or beautiful, it doesn't mean that you're not."

Just Be You!

THEIR WIN IS NOT YOUR LOSS

One of the reasons Olivia is so successful is because she writes universally truthful songs about the challenges of being a young woman in today's world. In 'jealousy, jealousy' and 'obsessed', she is unflinchingly honest about how often she compares herself with others and how insecure this makes her feel. In 'pretty isn't pretty', she continues this theme of comparison, exploring the specific pressures to be beautiful in a world where beauty standards are constantly changing, and therefore out of reach. By acknowledging these feelings so many of us have, Olivia puts them under a magnifying glass so we can see them for what they really are. She reminds us that comparison only holds us back, because we can never fully appreciate our own lives if we feel we're constantly in competition with other people. We are all on different paths, and we are all equally worthy of love and respect.

Just Be You!

NEVER LOSE SIGHT OF WHO YOU ARE

As one of the most famous people on the planet, Olivia could easily live a life of extreme self-importance and insist that people feed her grapes from a solid-gold platter (and we wouldn't blame her). But our Olivia prefers to stay grounded in the real world, like the rest of us normies: she's a big fan of riding on rental bikes and doing the newspaper crossword. As much as the glitz and the glamor can be appealing and even intoxicating, Olivia knows that there's even greater joy to be found in the simple things—and we couldn't agree more. Whether that's hanging out with your siblings, crocheting a scarf, going on a run, or jumping in the sea, ensure you always make time for those activities (and people) that make you feel alive, and most like yourself.

"Nobody can be perfect, ever."

Just Be You!

LET GO OF PERFECTION

Olivia has spent a lot of time contemplating what "perfect" means, and all the different ways to achieve it—writing the "perfect" album, buying makeup to create the "perfect" face, or becoming the "perfect" teen pop-star. However, she also knows that imperfection is a necessary part of being human—and sometimes the best things come from the most imperfect moments. Without her imperfect relationships and imperfect emotions, we'd never have the albums we know and love so much. Through her songs, Olivia reminds us that it's okay to say the wrong thing and stumble over our words sometimes. It's okay to have the best intentions, and for things not to work out how you hoped. It's okay to have chipped nail polish and to shout about the things that annoy you. It's okay to feel bad about yourself occasionally, so long as you still know, deep down, that you are more than enough.

Editor Millie Acers
Designer Isabelle Merry
Senior Production Editor Jennifer Murray
Senior Production Controller Louise Minihane
Senior Acquisitions Editor Pete Jorgensen
Managing Art Editor Jo Connor
Art Director Charlotte Coulais
Publisher Paula Regan
Managing Director Mark Searle
Written by Arielle Steele
Cover and interior illustrations Nastka Drabot
Additional artwork Isabelle Merry

DK would like to thank Alessandro Bessy
for copyediting and Victoria Taylor
for proofreading.

First published in Great Britain in 2025 by
Dorling Kindersley Limited
20 Vauxhall Bridge Road,
London SW1V 2SA

The authorised representative in the EEA is
Dorling Kindersley Verlag GmbH. Arnulfstr. 124,
80636 Munich, Germany

Copyright © 2025 Dorling Kindersley Limited
DK, a Division of Penguin Random House LLC
25 26 27 28 29 10 9 8 7 6 5 4 3 2 1
001–350206-Sep/2025

No part of this publication may be used or reproduced
in any manner whatsoever for the purpose of training artificial
intelligence technologies or systems. In accordance with
Article 4(3) of the DSM Directive 2019/790, DK expressly
reserves this work from the text and data mining exception.

All rights reserved. Without limiting the rights under the
copyright reserved above, no part of this publication may
be reproduced, stored in or introduced into a retrieval
system, or transmitted, in any form, or by any means
(electronic, mechanical, photocopying, recording, or
otherwise), without the prior written permission of the
copyright owner.

A CIP catalogue record for this book
is available from the British Library.
ISBN 978-0-2417-4529-8

Printed and bound in Slovakia

www.dk.com

Quotations: **p.6–7** "A New Decade, A New Album, A New Life—Olivia Rodrigo's Next Chapter", *Vogue*, Jia Tolentino, 2023; **p.8** "Olivia Rodrigo Burns Her Lips While Eating Spicy Wings", *Hot Ones*, Sean Evans, 2021; **p.10** "Olivia Rodrigo: Vampire, GUTS, and A New Era", *Bru On The Radio*, Josh Brubaker, 2023; **p.12** "Olivia Rodrigo on 'deja vu' & Her Top Songwriting Tips", *MTV News*, 2021; **p.14** "Olivia Rodrigo Talks Piano Lessons, School Life and Songwriting", *MTV UK*, 2021; **p.15** "Olivia Rodrigo: 'GUTS', 'get him back!', & Tour", *Apple Music*, Zane Lowe, 2023; **p.18** "Close Up: Olivia Rodrigo", *The Face*, Jade Wickes, 2021; **p.19** "10 Things Olivia Rodrigo Can't Live Without", *GQ*, 2023; **p.20** "Olivia Rodrigo and Phoebe Bridgers Let It All Out", *Interview*, Phoebe Bridgers, 2023; **p.21** "Olivia Rodrigo on 'deja vu' & Her Top Songwriting Tips", *MTV News*, 2021; **p.22** "'I had all these feelings of rage I couldn't express': Olivia Rodrigo on overnight pop superstardom, plagiarism and growing up in public", *The Guardian*, Laura Snapes, 2023; **p.24** "Olivia Rodrigo Was Built 4 This", *GQ*, Gabriella Paiella, 2021; **p.25** "Olivia Rodrigo: 'I'm a teenage girl. I feel heartbreak and longing really intensely'", *The Guardian*, Laura Snapes, 2021; **p.26** "Olivia Rodrigo Rates Heartbreak, High Heels, and Going To Therapy", *Pitchfork*, 2023; **p.30** "Olivia Rodrigo on 'GUTS' Album, Having a Hot Girl Summer, Living in New York City", *SiriusXM*, Davis Burleson, 2023; **p.32** "'I had all these feelings of rage I couldn't express': Olivia Rodrigo on overnight pop superstardom, plagiarism and growing up in public", *The Guardian*, Laura Snapes, 2023; **p.34** "Olivia Rodrigo on Cardi B, Feeling Powerful, and Her Dream Role", *Elle*, 2021; **p.36–37** "Olivia Rodrigo Describes the Heartbreak That Inspired Her Album *Sour*", *The Drew Barrymore Show*, Drew Barrymore, 2022; **p.38** "Olivia Rodrigo Was Built 4 This", *GQ*, Gabriella Paiella, 2021; **p.42** "Olivia Rodrigo *Sour* Interview", *Zach Sang Show*, Zach Sang, 2021; **p.43** "Olivia Rodrigo Describes the Heartbreak That Inspired Her Album *Sour*", *The Drew Barrymore Show*, Drew Barrymore, 2022; **p.43** "Olivia Rodrigo Is in the Driver's Seat", *The Face*, Lizzie Widdicombe, 2021; **p.43** "Olivia Rodrigo knows what makes her happy now", *The Face*, Jade Wickes, 2023; **p.44** "Olivia Rodrigo: 'vampire', New Album 'GUTS' & Moving to New York" *Apple Music*, Zane Lowe, 2023; **p.45** "73 Questions With Olivia Rodrigo", *Vogue*, 2023; **p.45** "Olivia Rodrigo: 'SOUR', 'drivers license,' and Performing Live", *Apple Music*, 2021; **p.46** "Olivia Rodrigo - Get To Know Me", *Olivia Rodrigo*, 2021; **p.48** Live onstage at the Guts Tour in Los Angeles, 2023; **p.49** *Instagram* (video), 2024; **p.50** "Olivia Rodrigo talks 'Vampire', Being A Pisces, How Lorde's Song Royals Inspired Her & MORE!", *102.7KIISFM*, 2023; **p.54** "Olivia Rodrigo: 'SOUR,' 'drivers license,' and Performing Live", *Apple Music*, 2021; **p.56** "Olivia Rodrigo talks 'Vampire', Being A Pisces, How Lorde's Song Royals Inspired Her & MORE!", *102.7KIISFM*, 2023; **p.57–58** "Olivia Rodrigo *Sour* Interview", *Zach Sang Show*, Zach Sang, 2021; **p.60** "Olivia Rodrigo talks Moving to New York, "Vampire", and New Album "GUTS", *104.3 MYfm*, Jon Comouche, 2023; **p.62** "'I had all these feelings of rage I couldn't express': Olivia Rodrigo on overnight pop superstardom, plagiarism and growing up in public", *The Guardian*, Laura Snapes, 2023

This book was made with Forest Stewardship Council™ certified paper – one small step in DK's commitment to a sustainable future.
Learn more at www.dk.com/uk/information/sustainability